The Garden of My Saying

The Garden of My Saying

Poems by

Daniel R. Schwarz

© 2025 Daniel R. Schwarz. All rights reserved.
This material may not be reproduced in any form, published,
reprinted, recorded, performed, broadcast,
rewritten or redistributed without
the explicit permission of Daniel R. Schwarz.
All such actions are strictly prohibited by law.

Cover design by Shay Culligan
Cover image by Marcia Jacobson
Author photo by Marcia Jacobson

ISBN: 978-1-63980-765-9

Kelsay Books
502 South 1040 East, A-119
American Fork, Utah 84003
Kelsaybooks.com

For my wife Marcia Jacobson, who makes so much possible; for my sons David Schwarz and Jeffrey Schwarz; and for generations of Cornell students whom I've had the privilege to teach.

Acknowledgments

I am indebted to my colleague Robert Morgan for taking seriously in the late 1980s and early 1990s my early efforts to write poetry.

I want to express appreciation to Vicky Brevetti, Gabriel Plaine, and Bryson Grygier for their continued assistance.

Morgan Perlstein's editorial help has been essential.

Thank you also to the following publications, in which versions of these poems previously appeared:

The Charlotte Poetry Review: "Depression's Vision"
Fogged Clarity: An Arts Review: "Closure," "Parallel (Paralyzed) Lives"
Hawaii Pacific Review: "Performance," "Tishah b'Ab," "Mene, Mene, Tekel Upharsin," "Rosh Hashanah," "Pentimento"
Humanities Review: "Rereading *Heart of Darkness*"
Ithaca Times: "Ocean Pleasures," "Raising Tomatoes," "February 2013," "Cancer: The Uninvited Guest," "Still Life: Raspberries, Apples, and a Sheet of Paper," "Perkins Cove, Ogunquit," "Jazz," "Life and Death on Black Oak Pond," "High Meadow, Keene Valley," "My Father's 84th Birthday," "Lobsterman at Porpoise Cove, Maine," "History Speaks," "Reading Texts, Reading Lives," "House Razing," "On Seeing a Family Friend for Perhaps the Last Time," "The Shape of Memory in Prague," "Words," "Strawberries," "Cornucopia," "Keene Valley," "Flying," "International Travel," "Credo at 66," "Ice Storm," "Looking Backwards at Eighty-Two: Anecdotes of Light and Dark," "Reading Dante's *The Divine Comedy*" "70th Birthday: A Self-Portrait," "Migration," "Pandemic Reflections," "Anecdote of the Bird Feeder," "Winter Thoughts," "Spring, 2005," "Daylight Savings Time"

Literary Laundry: "Broken Vows"
Marsh Hawk Press: "After My Father Died," "When I Was Thirty"
Memorial Volume for George Eickwort, ed. Sandy Lednor Padulka: "The Garden of Our Saying: Elegy for George"
Poem: "Tapestries," "Travel"
Rattle: "Elegy for Elizabeth Rose Lane Galloway," "Cindy at Schroon Lake"
Shofar: "Golem," "Utz"
Southern Humanities Review: "Remarriage"
Tailwind: "The Sarajevo Haggadah"
Weber Studies: "Charleston Lake, August, 1996," "James Thorpe's Daughter," "Cézanne in Philadelphia"
Westview: "Reading Joyce's *Ulysses,*" "Picasso's Women," "Blue Heron," "To My Only Brother: A Letter," "Generations," "The Muse Returns," "Spring Sounds," "The American Scholar," "Snowbound," "About Suffering," "Moon Blue," "Achievements by Others," "Pantomime," "Folly," "Fractured Expectations," "Mother in Hospice"

Contents

I. Speaking of Poetry

Words	15
Credo at 66	16
The American Scholar	17
Cataracts of Quotidian	18
History Speaks	19
When I Was Thirty	20
70th Birthday: A Self-Portrait	21
Tapestries	22

II. Sounds

Jazz	25
Spring Sounds	26

III. Between Divorce and Remarriage, 1984–1998

Closure	29
The Muse Returns	30
Migration	31
Parallel (Paralyzed) Lives	32
Broken Vows	33
Depression's Vision	34
Reading Texts, Reading Lives	35
Remarriage	36

IV. Family Matters

Mother in Hospice   39
My Only Brother: A Letter   41
My Father's 84th Birthday   42
After My Father Died   44

V. Nature Speaks

Still Life: Raspberries, Apples, and Sheet of Paper   47
Pentimento   48
February 2013   49
Pandemic Reflections   50
Winter Thoughts: Predetermined Patterns   52
Ice Storm   53
Moon Blue   54
Life and Death on Black Oak Pond   55
Cornucopia   56
Snowbound   57
Anecdote of the Bird Feeder   58
Blue Heron   59
Ocean Pleasures   60
Perkins Cove, Ogunquit   61
Charleston Lake, Ontario   62
Raising Tomatoes   63

VI. Exploring Jewish Heritage

Mene, Mene, Tekel Upharsin	67
Tisha B'Ab, 1993	68
Rosh Hashanah, 1994	69
The Sarajevo Haggadah	70
The Shape of Memory in Prague	71
Golem	72

VII. Portraits

Lobsterman at Porpoise Cove, Maine	75
Utz	76
House Razing	78
James Thorpe's Daughter	80

VIII. Portraits (II): Elegies

The Garden of Our Saying: Elegy for George	83
On Seeing a Family Friend for the Last Time	85
Cindy at Schroon Lake	86
Performance	87
Elegy for Elizabeth Rose Lane Galloway	89
Generations	91
Cancer: The Uninvited Guest	93

IX. Briefly: Haiku

Nature	97
Questions of Travel	98
Perspectives	100

X. The Mind's Garden: Imaginative Journeys

Travel	103
Looking Backwards at Eighty-Two: Anecdotes of Light and Dark	104
Possessions	107
Reading Dante's *The Divine Comedy*	108
Reading Joyce's *Ulysses*	110
About Suffering	112
Cézanne in Philadelphia	113
Picasso's Women	115
On (Re)Reading Tolstoy's *War and Peace*	116
Rereading Conrad's *Heart of Darkness*	117

XI. Conclusion

Fragrant Portals	121

I. Speaking of Poetry

Words

Words are my mind's mirror,
editing what I see of self and world,
transforming brine in which ideas soak:
imagination's amanuensis and muse,
giving shape to what might be.
Words are nets
in which I try to catch
swimming ephemera of my life;
while I have woven them tight,
from filaments of experience,
I do not always know how to set the nets
to catch tortured thoughts, tender feelings.
Words are closets and drawers
where I put my things,
ordering tentatively life's disorder;
honing tools to shape inchoate thoughts;
putty to fill insignificant gaps
where tiny drafts penetrate;
whetstones to sharpen memory;
intricate mosaics shaped by experience
into elaborate patterns.
Words are memory's archaeology
by which I excavate my past,
recalling or creating
lost visions of childhood,
capturing evanescent dreams. Words are
nocturnal fictions of fulfillment,
undoing day's fantasies.
Words are soul's music,
tongue's plaything,
mind's geometry,
default landscape of my soul.

Credo at 66

To write one must feel: I believe
passionately in possibility of
romantic love, communication,
intimacy. I have joyful,
affirmative feelings—but am moved by
aging, reversal, loneliness.

My ideal writing voice: enthusiasm
tempered with judgment, generously
trying to understand others;
respectful of language's
potential to create precision and felt responses;
open to possibilities of life, empathetic;
romantic in the best sense:
knowing life is gift we should cherish.

My diction: dialogue of diverse
influences—erudite, nostalgic,
sensuous, academic, cosmopolitan,
Jewish, urban, perhaps even
worldly, but—notwithstanding
decades of sustained reading, travel,
museums (punctuated by wrenching
divorce, loss, sadness)—
always touched by tomorrow's hope.

The American Scholar

The world is his who can see through its pretension.
—Ralph Waldo Emerson, "The American Scholar"

"Write a simple, happy poem;
your pain bores me."
"I can't write what I don't feel."
"Had you any sense, you would
not write your damned poems
of gloom and doom.
Write a romantic love poem,
speak of lovely moon,
changing colors of October leaves,
red sunset hovering on Lake Cayuga."
"Ah, but when I feel fine frenzy of a poem,
my emotions overwhelm me
like incoming tide surging over sand.
I need to chew on bones of experience,
drink dregs of bitterness,
taste ashes of regret."

Cataracts of Quotidian

How do we avoid
cataracts of quotidian,
responding as we always have,
thinking in clichés,
seeing with blinders,
understanding fresh and
new only in rote terms of
what we have been taught?

History Speaks

September 11, 2001

History thrusts its horrors on television.
Planes flying into World Trade Center,
massacring helpless victims, destroying buildings,
fragmenting family histories.
Desperately searching, rescuers discover
hieroglyphs of death: charred carnage,
smashed corpses of those who jumped,
unreachable voices beneath rubble.

As a boy, I saw
history's malevolent wink:
a collision of two commuter trains.
Tightly holding my mother's hand
I stood transfixed, helpless to intervene,
as smoke curled into dusk,
acrid smell of scorched human flesh.
Even today etched images still live of
twisted metal, maimed bodies,
transforming wives into widows,
depriving my playmates of fathers.

Conflagration of skin and bone: the Holocaust.
Escaping extermination by geographical accident,
trying to enter horrors that
resist language, yet require words,
I retrieve shards of buried world,
remnants of indifferent history
echoing in nightmares, whispers.

When I Was Thirty

When I was thirty, I thought
what I did, I would do again;
every place I visited would be
overture to symphony of returns.
Savoring my everyday
dishes of experience
as if they were *foie gras,*
the world seemed an endless banquet,
extravagant confection.
But now it is otherwise.
When I leave place or play
could this be my
final call? Take my recent trip to
London, where I seemed magnetically
drawn to reminders of mortality. Will I
behold again Holbein's trompe-l'œil
The Ambassadors, with its
death's-head mirror of
my vanitas? Once more revel in
splendid St. Paul's touched by fire or
Parthenon remnants in British Museum?
That sense of infinite possibility decades ago
gives way to Time's inevitable advances.
I mourn books I'll never write, cities I
shall never walk, fabled novels
I'll never read, lush paintings
I have missed or
hardly given more than glance,
knowing then I would return.
Mortality's arrow quivers in my flesh.

70th Birthday: A Self-Portrait

May 12, 2011

Contours of my life already drawn,
lines determined, prime colors
set off by
background combinations;
impasto, shading,
lighting (chiaroscuro).
Mostly finished: balance with
tinge of excess, flair here,
incongruity there. Small areas of
undefined negative space await
deft hand of ensuing years,
touching up slight inconsistencies,
dark spots that need clarification,
but not without possibility
of major reconfiguring.

Tapestries

I love woven tapestries,
comprehensible fabrics of harmony;
especially those with
loose, tattered thread
yet still
coherent in form.
I study asymmetry
in warp and woof,
irregularity in Persian carpets,
faded colors in wall hangings.
A man of rough, ragged edges,
I appreciate life's tatters, rips, and tears.

II. Sounds

Jazz

All that
jazz
syn
  co co
    pa pa pat
      tion
enerrrgy
s
  l
    iiii
   d
   e
trommmbone,
m-u-u-u-t-t-ed
blare, flare
brassy, sassy
trumpet;
bum de mum,
rum a tum
of drums;
rambunctious
rhythm
of
d
y
ing
feelings.
S(Z)ounds!

Spring Sounds

Spring sounds:
low-pitched baritone
of roaring creek, insistently,
slowly cutting shapes as it
gathers its strength,
rolls, tumbles, roaring
strongly in bass,
then, yes, tenor surge
over ancient rocks
in three discrete small cataracts,
before coalescing at next plateau
returning to orderly pattern,
softer, gentler gurgling
of soprano trickles and alto drips,
pleasurable cacophonous trilling.

III. Between Divorce and Remarriage, 1984–1998

Closure

1985

"You're interrupting
my radio," she said,
as I fell into my easy
chair, turned on TV,
seeking respite
from noise in images.
Divorce: ours
more like slow
tearing of limb
than surgical amputation,
more drifting
apart than cataclysm.
Was it ever
passionate attraction
that tightens chest,
magnetizes eyes? Rather,
more moving
together gradually
to soothe needs, as if
burying head under
comforter on blustery
dark December night
awaiting dawn's
inevitability.

The Muse Returns

"I am in elegiac mood,
nostalgic for what should have been,
anxious to mourn days gone by,
to find paths not taken,
words not said;
I need to drink from dregs of regret and loss."
"Let us not live in the world of
what if or might have been
or I should have and could have,
and almost or but.
She's gone and it's time to build a tomorrow."
"I need to scold and blame myself and suffer
romantic agony."
"Ah poor man,
there you go again.
Revel in the world's
delicious cornucopia of pleasures;
each day is your
harvest, banquet, and bouquet."

Migration

I was captivated by
a preening, wooing,
weathered woman,
sitting on her high branch,
voicing deep-throated
warbles on a warm spring day.
She was surprise gift
to my middle years.
But migratory birds
soon depart
to make new nests.

Parallel (Paralyzed) Lives

Cooking naked:
seasoning salmon fillets:
olive oil, oregano,
lemon juice, black pepper;
I shave asparagus stalks,
she tosses salad.
Dancing as one, we
revel in soft gazes, urgent touches,
tongues respond with bluesy kisses,
sounds in our throats as
sighs cross desires.
At dawn our music ceases.

Broken Vows

1991

Did *you* hear the silent sounds:
echoes, whispers, gestures of
broken promises, evasions,
telling omissions?
I heard *your* steps
on both sides of the street,
juggling life to
fit opportunity.

Depression's Vision

1993

Herein did the shape of evil dip his hand and prepare to lay the mark of baptism upon their foreheads, that they might be partakers of the mystery of sin, more conscious of the secret guilt of others, both indeed and thought, than they could be now of their own.
—Nathaniel Hawthorne, *Young Goodman Brown*

There came a time that—
like Goodman Brown,
another who knew God's ways,
found in prayer's darkness,
reflections of night's shadows—
she could see past nature's wonders,
beauty of autumn leaves turning,
red sunset hovering on lake
before its evening disappearance,
could forget
moments of tenderness,
warmth of a shared bed,
know my secret guilt—
my sins in word and deed
or—isn't that our curse?—thought she could.

Reading Texts, Reading Lives

I wired blue flowers
in the shape of a guitar
with a message:
"Woman in Sunshine:
after the final No
there comes a Yes.
I love you passionately;
forgive me;
keep hope alive,
the Man with the Blue Guitar."
A few weeks passed.
Her response:
"It's too late;
time will not relent.
I wish you well,
but I am not it.
Mrs. Alfred Uruguay."
Alas, we begin and
end with Stevens.

Remarriage

1998

Wrung, wrinkled by time,
ringed by custom, wrought by need,
we converge, yet keep our individual markers,
bumps and potholes etched by prior journeys.
Our places on life's map already drawn,
unlike decades ago,
when I and another
Marcia carved and curved
other roads with our sons. Now
country roads winding
through familiar venues—
let us say the Poconos,
or perhaps the Berkshires—retrace
the geography of memory,
meshing portals of discovery
with inns where bodies briefly sang.
Remarriage after mid-life is more
a circumnavigation than a thruway.
On sailing days we are Magellans
sharing new discoveries of self,
revisiting past lives:
flashes of recognition, nuances of regret.
On port days, we need remember,
as routines fall into place,
to forget compass, discard maps,
let intuition dance.

IV. Family Matters

Mother in Hospice

April 2005

"I am drowning," she mumbled,
"I am ready to die. I don't want
my family's lives in suspension."
But her mind was lucid.
Crowded into cubicle with
living remnants of her body,
four of us—
my taciturn brother who
put life on hold to be caregiver;
my second wife, Marcia,
who knew what to do and say;
my younger son, Jeff, who had never
seen death's color, texture;
myself, guilty for not doing more,
frustrated that doctors knew so little—
were, in her halting whisper,
counseled to love each other,
avoid strife, anger.
Her final words were who she was.
To my wife: "Take care of Danny."
Eyes close, few minutes silence:
"Marcia, you make wonderful rugelach.
How is your ailing father doing?"
To me: "You have found joy in
sharing interests with your wife." Pause.
"We need to find someone for you, Jeff."
With barely audible laughter,
she recalled defending me
to fifth grade teacher who
thought I was inattentive, even ironic:

"You were smarter than your teachers;
children need to laugh and have fun."

She taught us to die with grace and dignity.
"A great lady!" I tearfully told my son
as we watched her fight for breath,
"She was quite a beauty into her sixties;
is she not even more beautiful
radiating love for family?"
In intermittent moments of clarity,
she lived in fabric of
human feeling and memory.

She always knew what I have come to learn;
her lesson: savor small pleasures; smiles, touches;
sunrises, sunsets; cardinals feeding;
herons, deer visiting pond;
intimacies between tick and tock
when life momentarily blazes
are not mere interstices
but warp and woof of life itself.
Her favorite color was blue.

My Only Brother: A Letter

Montage: images of comity, conflict,
haunt my troubled dreams.
We have retreated to fortresses
of mutual suspicion, unyielding pride
built stone by stubborn stone;
it is not that you are Cain, and I, Abel.
Yet our boyhood ties
dissolved by an act of betrayal:
the acid of a misdirected letter—
motiveless malignity or green jealousy?—
leaving in my flesh
still quivering arrow,
festering wound
twisting memory
into misbegotten shapes.

My Father's 84th Birthday

My ghostperson:
that man whose photographs
ruefully draw my likeness,
whose former shape
is my shadow walking
thirty years before me,
taking last laps
at what seems to him
hectic pace,
but oh so slow to
those who watch.

His legs throb with pain;
blockage dams riverblood,
heartpower pumps slowly.
Yet talking is kind of action,
like golfing, fishing were once.
Incessantly humming, buzzing
about his own symptoms,
he doesn't really hear words,
just pitch of empty sounds,
encroaching upon attention.
Outline of who I will become,
mirror of future
written by past history

as wrinkles, wounds,
wisdom ancient—
or what passes for it.

As he blinks, shrinks, winks,
I see myself
as my children's shadow.

After My Father Died

Conversational Sonnet, 2005

Father's death: anger thawed. No longer stuck
in iciness of recurring nightmares.
Mother's death gave way to
gracious tingle of forgiveness.
Gradually sweeter child memories
melted surface: catching fish, playing catch,
watching him excel in adult softball,
embarrassedly hearing weird shrill
whistle (calling us as if we were his dogs),
balancing himself parallel to ground
as he wrapped his arms around street pole.
Ample knowledge, prolix advice,
displayed in flamboyant explanations:
teaching what he knew needed to be known.

V. Nature Speaks

Still Life: Raspberries, Apples, and Sheet of Paper

Signatures we are here to read:
something about fleshy, fruity, red, fall raspberries,
seductively inviting
us to sate lush craving:
rough textured and rare,
even iconoclastic,
oozing juice to fortunate touch, leaving
tinctures, stains, on disheveled clothes,
responding to gentlest touch of tongue,
to licks of pleasure,
encrypting their mark, their signature
on whatever they touch.
It is otherwise with apples:
crunchy, resistant, aromatic, tart;
or with sweet flavor
that lingers on tongue
almost with cloying taste.
Juice stored in huge cider vats
offering its democratic pleasures
to those whose palates
appreciate slow autumnal
rhythms of nature's harvest
and country nectars.

Pentimento

Like faded or skewed memory,
faint colors, blurred lines
of pentimento appear in oblique form,
not quite painted over, and not quite there.
Meanderings in Rome:
a Caravaggio, unexpectedly discovered,
which refused to reveal in the dark
faint images beneath the Virgin;
an intimate shared moment,
of words not spoken
because there was no need,
of chances missed,
affirmations shadowed by doubt,
reconciling incomplete,
resolutions unke(m)pt.
December is month of pentimento.
Bare branches speak of loss, past loves,
unfulfilled possibilities,
awkward touching, yet alone
like fruit that does not ripen.

Corridors of memory:
little shames like rashes on our mind,
searing actualities turned to dust,
or sweet regrets, piquant on memory's palette,
aftertaste
of delicate pastry or fine wine,
or mingled bodies,
painted over
pages, days, tales
that no longer come into focus.

February 2013

Internal rhythm of lengthening
February days: at close of
exquisite winter day when
sun shone brightly on glistening
snow, knife-like icicles hung from
white birches, brilliant sunset painted sky
blue-red, I wound my way back through
rolling hills from Syracuse—past frightened
deer, hungry squirrels, two dead raccoons—
always in tune with setting sun.

Pandemic Reflections

December 2020

I have traveled a good deal in Concord.
    —Henry David Thoreau, *Walden*

Daily winter walks
slow down pace of life,
bring inner peace, joy.
One day: crimson sunset
giving way to multi-colored
skyscape in late afternoon,
accompanied by sounds
of rain-filled creek
tumbling over rocks.
Nature's drama:
hungry deer stretch
on hind legs to feast
at bird feeder;
predatory Cooper's Hawk
sits high in birch tree,
awaiting small birds,
while squirrels
traverse fields.
First snow, glistening
in odd patterns,
blankets leafless trees.
Silence, stasis replace
usual ebb and flow.
Next day spectacular site:
melting snow nurtures
cascading waterfalls
into gorges below.
Snowshoeing past
our frozen pond,

I ponder my
interior weather:
what awaits in
woods' shadows
as I approach eighty?
Such reflections challenge,
but do not impede,
December's pleasures.

Winter Thoughts: Predetermined Patterns

December 21, 2021

A three-hundred-year-old white oak tree
survives the elements: casting shadows,
its statuesque bare branches
puts senses at their mercy,
stimulates memory's
shorter, cooler days.
As the year winds down,
I walk in damp, darkening
woods, buffeted by chilling
wind, alive to different
shapes of leafless trees,
roaring sounds of full brooks
foraging squirrels, chipmunks.
I behold a brilliant Turner
skyscape: dollops of passion's bright
red, gentle touches of pale blue,
incipient threatening black
punctuate orange.
Hasn't it has always
been like this, my seeking narrative patterns
amidst the marshes of my mind?
Battered veteran of interior autumns,
branches and leaves stripped bare,
external decay that will not repair,
I too prepare for another spring.

Ice Storm

Roads closed,
power down,
encased cars.
Icicles press
on trees, wires.
Indoors:
crackling fire
arouses sensuality,
awakens desire.

Moon Blue

Huge, brilliant, gold disc
against sable night,
its phosphorescent brightness
walking on rocky edge.
Fat moon crouches heavily
over mountain, backwoods;
snowdrifts touch its fullness
swelling like pregnant woman.
Moonlight crystals burst
flaming on white evergreens,
as if winking at snow's abstract patterns,
etched by winnowing wind and snowshoes;
winking, too, at the aspen: scarred,
mottled with deadly red blight,
dappled grey, umber.
Moon blue seemed to bide its time
as if it were this once, this very once,
not to set, to recede, be overtaken
but rather stop us in our hurry
to watch its lighting, its birthing.

Life and Death on Black Oak Pond

Nine tiny ducklings
closely follow their mother,
swimming on a dense layer
of green algae; in pond's center
lies a fly-infested doe carcass,
floating legs up. We
extract the corpse, with help
of poles, ropes, and a
grizzled wild-animal expert
who himself got stuck in the mud.
Our work disturbed a knot of
baby ducks, now circled
'round their watchful mother,
indifferent to nature's
other rhythms and the
human comedy twenty yards away.

Cornucopia

What summer raspberries are to sexuality,
fall apples are to mortality.
Whether green or russet or pied,
crispy, sour, hard, or chewy,
they feel of incipient autumn,
shorter days, grown children.
Cider is juice of middle age,
tart, tangy, and easily fermented.
Raspberries are to moment
what apples are to nostalgia.
Green succulent asparagus,
with brushy grainy flexible heads,
atop proud stiff reeds
stimulate memory of prior seasons:
artichokes offer opulent pleasures
within moist leaves.
Ripe rich summer tomatoes
resonate with redness of sunset.
Pale green honeydew melons
proffer soft lush whitish center;
sweet cantaloupes anticipate
bright orange yams, which play
their part in holiday rituals.

Snowbound

> *His soul swooned slowly as he heard the snow falling faintly through the universe and faintly falling, like the descent of their last end, upon all the living and the dead.*
> —James Joyce, *"The Dead"*

As far as eye can see,
quiet as pure white,
peaceful as country landscape,
still as frozen pond. Snow
bends trees and ragged bushes,
blankets earth, buries roads,
homogenizes houses,
nullifies difference.
Blizzard awakens my soul.
It's as if I were enclosed in womb
from which I emerge reborn,
or crypt that magically reopens.
Smoldering passion, creativity, curiosity,
melt snow, prepare
ground for flowering, renewal.

Anecdote of the Bird Feeder

Like Stevens's jar in Tennessee,
our metal feeder
took dominion everywhere,
transformed, magnetized
towering leafless birch into
winter alms station.
Hierarchies soon followed
on heel of custom:
jealousy, greed, wariness,
deference to size, to gender, to fierceness;
lyrical mockingbirds await
their turn on upper branches,
deferring to imposing
blue jays. Strutting female cardinals,
—overshadowed by their mates' red beauty—
co-exist, perhaps uneasily,
with chickadees, finches,
only to give way to
huge, ominous crows,
while fearful warblers, woodpeckers,
grudgingly concede spillage
to chipmunks, squirrels, deer.

Blue Heron

Florida, 2000

Canoeing, my wife and I
gasped at blue heron
presiding over marshes,
majestically balanced,
gently arched, purple
"S"-shaped neck,
delicate grey-green
razor thin legs on tiny branch
jutting into swamp.
As we quietly approached, it
gloriously took flight
landing ten yards in front of us.
This became a pattern: our pursuits,
its abbreviated low flight to another spot,
always in front until
we turned towards dock
when it hovered behind;
we backpaddled to catch a final glance.

When we later saw our heron
(or another larger great blue one?)
soar on enormous wing,
heard its mating honk,
I was reminded how we fear
the incomprehensible
as we seek narrative patterns
amidst the marshes of our generations.

Ocean Pleasures

We walk beyond the genius of the sea,
cherishing dunes covered with sea oats.
Tide's small white eruptions
punctuate blue vista.
Sandpipers, gulls barely stir
as we stand beside one another,
enjoying surging white foam;
warning red flags
reduce us to cautious wading.
Outstretched fishing pier dotted
with expectant anglers greeting
rising sun before mid-day reality:
"Fishing does not mean catching,"
someone says, as someone always does,
while another washes caught redfish,
tosses innards back to the sea.
At twilight red clouds streaked with orange
trace patched blue-brown sunset on horizon.
As it has always been for me,
smell of fish, children baiting hooks
under watchful eyes,
shimmering waves,
odd shapes and bold colors
(disrupting purity of Boudin seascape)
give ocean definition as human pleasure.

Perkins Cove, Ogunquit

June 1996

I hear ocean music of my childhood
moaning against ruins of ancient rocks,
giant brown stones left by glaciers. Life
leaves its detritus.
As we walk hand in hand
on Marginal Way, savoring memories
of fat red lobsters,
mussels by the dozen,
and smell of fresh cooked fish,
dawn pushes back darkness;
ebb tide reaches towards its turn,
chokes estuary with sand.
Gently touching, we saunter
along the shore, aware of
ducks washed by breaking ripples. Now:
not raging waves of adolescent passion,
storms of young adulthood ambition,
rather motion of graying middle years,
quiet rolling, slower days,
sunsets.

Charleston Lake, Ontario

August 1996

I caught at dawn
hummingbirds,
drawn by dime store plastic red feeder.
The whirling whirr of wings,
a sound much larger than themselves,
fills the morning air.
A dark needle beak
inhales sugary morsel,
facsimile of flower nectar.
Wary red-headed one,
more regal than the rest,
approaches, takes startled peek,
rejects my presence,
beats its wings,
turns, departs.

Fragile birds,
needing constant nourishment,
always a few hours from death,
stopping to feed, soon leaving:
images of ourselves,
seeking, inhaling pleasure,
enjoying this, that,
whirring our whir
before departing.

Raising Tomatoes

Our summer guests: friends,
children came and went,
stayed a few days, shared meals.
Cupid, Sweet 100, Rutgers,
Early Girl, Best Boy, Cherokee Purple
arrived in late May
as seedling tykes,
stayed the season,
growing to ripe succulent maturity,
yielding at different times to harvest:
diverse community, hybrid and heritage:
yellow, purple, shades of red;
wildly different in size: cherry, grape;
smaller, full-sized;
all rich with blossoms.

They took dominion everywhere.
Eight feet vines reached upward
sprawling bushes on deck,
tentacles wrapping around railings,
or intruding like
recalcitrant neighbors,
into each other's space
until restrained by stakes and string,
finally coming together
as orchestrated vegetation.
Like pets or children, they
required nurturing, then schooling,
feeding, protection
against vicissitudes of fungus, insects,

to ensure the blossoms set
until, overcoming spasms of drought,
more rain than needed, hail, heat, cold,
marred by cracks, blemishes, discoloration,
they reach graduation: abundantly
fulfilling their fruity potential,
before dying at first hard frost.

VI. Exploring Jewish Heritage

Mene, Mene, Tekel Upharsin

In the same hour came forth fingers of a man's hand and wrote over against the candlestick upon the plaster of the wall of the king's palace; and the king saw the palm of the hand that wrote.
—The Book of Daniel

Awestruck, I stopped,
to once again be dazzled by
Rembrandt's *Belshazzar's Feast*.
I imagine a drunken
Belshazzar among his roistering subjects
drinking from sacred vessels
plundered by his father Nebuchadnezzar
at destruction of the
Temple in Jerusalem.
I see him stare in amazed fear
at strange words on wall
written by disembodied hand
appearing mysteriously:
Mene, Mene, Tekel Upharsin.
My namesake translated these words in Aramaic:
"Numbered, numbered, weighed, and divided."
I too am interpreter of odd texts,
strange narratives of my life:
two or three women
of other cultures, other ways,
leaving their writing on my wall
in languages I cannot understand.
I, Daniel, have been summoned
to read their signs—and they mine.
They have numbered, divided
my days, and I theirs.

Tisha B'Ab, 1993

Tisha B'Ab is a fast day on the ninth day of the Hebrew month Ab, commemorating the destruction of the First and Second Temples, at the hands of the Babylonians in 586 B.C. and six centuries later in 70 A.D. by the Romans.

It was on Tisha B'Ab that my second temple fell:
"I'm leaving; I'm on empty and have no more to give."
Since my midlife divorce—the destruction, alas,
of my first temple—
I have always had mournful feelings
on that hot muggy day in summer
when Orthodox Jews fast, and
Sephardic Jews wear black jellabas.

Yet do I not now recall in remote Toraja
on eighth day of Hannukah, Festival of Light,
we lit candles on my simple aluminum menorah
where perhaps no Jews had been before?
Full of expectation and adventure, we
drove ten hours on a pitted road
to visit sacred burial rites,
culminating in animal sacrifice,
pyre of funeral buildings.

My spare hotel room
became holy temple;
as nine candles blazed;
I imagine I walk
along sacred Wailing Wall of
Solomon's Ancient Temple,
believing that another
temple always rises.

Rosh Hashanah, 1994

I beheld solitary blue heron,
with its drooping plumage,
standing by my pond,
oblivious to sound, unaware that
its odd beauty came from
El Grecoesque
exaggerated bill,
elongated neck,
reedy legs.
Suddenly in one
swooping motion,
it dove, returning
to its station
with a blue gill.
Once more reminded
of how nature's grim
equilibrium
rhymes with its beauty,
I felt New Year's inevitable
oscillating cycle
of hope and disappointment in
heron's dazzling swoop,
and stillness of our pond.

The Sarajevo Haggadah

"Bosnia Jews Glimpse Book and Hope"
—*New York Times* headline, April 16, 1995

Marked with smudges,
children's scrawls,
richly colored illustrations—
the Creation,
Moses blessing the Israelites—
frail vellum,
wine stains of six hundred
years of peregrinations.
Exodus and Diaspora:
testament
to perseverance, resilience,
deliverance.
Mysteriously re-appearing,
as if sent to Passover seder
by Elijah in his stead,
speaking of Jews
persecuted in Egypt,
bearing scars
of its own diaspora
from Northern Spain;
surviving intermittent
shelling, civil strife,
this Haggadah
tells and tolls
its history in Sarajevo,
ancient suffering land.

The Shape of Memory in Prague

Once again, I learn
what *Shoah* means.
In synagogue, now a museum,
I examine children's
art from Terezin—
dark gray, heavy lines;
mysterious large intrusive shapes—and
photographs of their creators;
I feel bound to those
sad, dark-eyed victims,
knowing I belong
to an ancient people
that stared down
obliteration,
outlived death camps.

Golem

The Maharal of Prague,
Rabbi Loew,
created golem out of clay
by means of cabalistic rite
to protect Jewish ghetto
from siege.
If potter's wheel could make a
figure to keep our hurts at bay,
if only we could
breathe life into clay to
keep safe illusions,
shield our children,
ward off wounds, and
protect feelings from injury.
Yet we need remember
that nothing is simple.
When his golem ran amuck,
the Maharal had it destroyed.

VII. Portraits

Lobsterman at Porpoise Cove, Maine

Summer 1996

"About a hundred years,"
he said, anticipating my question,
as he stood on the dock, proudly bent
above shabby, barnacled boat,
hip-booted, dressed in layered clothing
more suited to chilled spring dawn
than July's oppressive summer sun.
On timeworn pulley system,
he hauled lobster pots
for repair from winter's ravages,
working in silent tandem with his brother below,
each aware of necessary motions.
While fingering torn wires of his pots,
he glanced proudly into noon haze:
"Ours are the red flags with circle M,
but we all know whose pots are whose."
Pleased that my interest
took a quiet bent,
he clipped words
as if for him expenditure of language
were more weary work than hauling pots.
"Last load up."
Finally, quarry: red-brown crustaceans:
captives wiggling, wriggling,
seeking water, space.
Squinting eyes surveyed the catch:
"Not much today."

Utz

> *Utz was the owner of a spectacular collection of Meissen porcelain which, through his adroit maneuvers, had survived the Second World War and the years of Stalinism in Czechoslovakia.*
>
> —Bruce Chatwin, *Utz*

I met him after visiting
Stockholm synagogue
on a June *Shabbat*
on year's longest day. "I'm a collector,"
then a pause,
"of ancient Chinese artifacts."
I turned to voice in what
I believed an empty room of
Stockholm Museum of Far Eastern Antiquities.
"I too am a collector," I thought, hearing
mysterious stranger. This time:
a man about my height and age
dressed also in black, a short, slightly stooped,
angular figure of middle years,
pronounced pointed nose, preternaturally thin,
concave chest, and hollowed cheeks;
Giacometti's *Walking Man,*
bent, carved by experience and history.
By unspoken rapport that
develops among those who obsessively
frequent museums, he became my guide,
speaking in imperfect English about ancient
Chinese pots and statues, admiring details of one,
declaring another "not quite as good."
His eyes blazed with passion.

In him, I saw figures
who had approached me in Europe
when a twenty-one-year-old student: survivors
collecting me, fellow Jew, reminder of lost
sons, brothers.
Were it not for my probing,
he would have shared nothing about himself:
his father had volunteered to fight Franco.
When I asked if he was a
Jew, he responded, "I am a Marxist-Leninist,
but I go to the April Holocaust service.
We survived Terezin,
but following 1968 purges, I left
Prague thirty years ago with mother."
Marked by history like Chinese antiquities,
his face seemed etched with shifting
map of twentieth century Europe.
Divorced, lonely, cautious, yet intimate,
he spoke haltingly of painful
visits to daughter in Rome.
He was the connoisseur, my Utz,
but was I not collecting this cadaverous
treasure from archives of lost Jewish Europe
for my memory and imagination?
We parted without exchanging names.

House Razing

for Margaret Anne, Huntsville, Alabama

Flame ebbs, smoke clears;
we stare at charred remnants of rafters,
foundation stones,
two chimneys amidst ruins,
stairs to nowhere,
broken glass, ashes, shards.
More: tattered clothes, torn mattresses,
overturned swing, carriage remnants,
rusted, derelict cars
among huge shade trees.
Scattered bricks
mark history of house that
stood when Union army crisscrossed
Northern Alabama.
A serviceable abode
nurturing inhabitants, reaching decrepitude:
a living organism with
muscles, tendons, nerves, and
bones peeking through flaccid skin.
My companion stands alone,
her pale fragility outlasting its wood frame.
History is writ in her ancient Jewish eyes,
wrinkled face, graying hair, seared memory:
last survivor of a homestead family
whose abandoned house now
attracts, like rusty magnet,
dispossessed squatters, vagrants.

After execution, dumb show elegy:
we picnic silently,
tasting dregs of wine,
staring at the burnt corpse.

James Thorpe's Daughter

You are the greatest athlete in the world.
—King Gustav of Sweden, 1912 Olympics

"May I show you his medals?"
Deeply lined, slightly stooped, she approached
our table, opened her bag, took out
faded ribbons, medals, certificates
signifying triumph of fleet and strong:
"I knew and didn't know my father."
"Few of us do," I thought, "yet we
carry their medals in worn wallets,
tattered handbags, of our memory."

At his quaint mausoleum in Mauch Chunk,
renamed Jim Thorpe, where
celebration in stone struggles
with time's drab weathering, I had
overheard gossip dismissing her
as a sad old woman clinging to
muted echoes of stories spun.

On a day in the mountains
when I found beauty in movement—
muskrats' slow poky probing, rustling leaves
of the statuesque red maples—I
realized her gift: resilient
withstanding storms of disappointment,
knitting felt knowledge from legend.

VIII. Portraits (II): Elegies

The Garden of Our Saying:
Elegy for George

for George Eickwort (1949–1994),
killed in an automobile accident
in Jamaica, The West Indies, July 11, 1994

I. Dissonance

It was as if it snowed in torrid summer,
or zinnias burst forth
with shriveled marigold buds,
or the caterpillars arrested their progress
into butterflies,
or as if cawing crow disrupted
katydid's summer song.

II. Three Days Later

On the morning
when I heard about
conflagration of metal and bone,
I saw solitary
lissome blue heron by my pond.
Long necked, catching sight of sunfish,
it snapped to attention—
but seemed to flag in its hereditary mission
for some mysterious reason
as if it knew of
terrible disruption
in nature's rhythm.
As unaware of his beauty
as zinnia or marigold,
George was Matisse among ordinary grey,
giving scintillant reds
to our being. Lamed Vov,
he justiced in his days, ways.

III. Memorial Service

We sat outdoors amidst
roses' scents, blooms,
speaking of what he meant,
like lobs slowly crossing,
re-crossing the net.
I felt impelled to speak of his
fundamental decency,
groped, g(r)asped for metaphors
as if seeking inspiration in
manicured garden of our obsequies.

IV. October Reminiscence: Three Months Later

With outburst energy, intermittent quiet,
in bright orange foliage of year
—my life's autumn?—he evokes
memory of that blue heron,
gangly legged walk,
head thrust forcefully forward
as if always on watch,
his long arms in motion
outstretched to ensnare butterflies
or retrieve elusive tennis balls—
or to reach for elusive
gifts of heart, mind.

On Seeing a Family Friend for the Last Time

for Mickey Friedman

No longer mobile, obese, her
legs thickened, scarred with blue-black bulging
veins, dressed in widow's black, tastefully
jeweled, her smile and dancing eyes speak
welcome to my visit; her makeup
disguises age, tries to emphasize tautness
of thin porcelain skin. Her delicate
hands rest in her lap surrounded by
heirlooms enhancing elegant
space: her relative Jacob Epstein's
sculptures; Hummel figurines; Wedgwood.

Sounds flutter as if moved by breath;
our voices, looks, gestures
relive playful and ceremonial gatherings.
Specters occupy room,
hover as we speak; conversations
weave customary texture,
like her worn Persian and Turkish rugs.
I, who will never occupy
a space for fifty years, hours before
meandered through my childhood home,
a block and an era away,
now overlaid with other gazes.

I rest on memory's rich upholstery.

Cindy at Schroon Lake

As we wander through fields
of your family homestead,
even after thirty long years
you search for past
traces in debris of
tennis court, softball field,
reclaimed by brush.
Seeing shards, remnants
of a collapsed backboard,
you think of
childhood play
of your late son
senselessly killed.
Images of my living sons
flash suddenly
as if our sons were at play
on these very grounds.

Performance

*for my student Christopher Reeve (1952–2004),
thrown by a horse May 27, 1995*

I.

I recall teaching you as "Chris,"
confident, articulate, ambitious—
scintillating peacock among brown wrens—
magnetizing young women
who dressed for your approval,
waiting to see where you would settle
before choosing their places.
Feeling the presence of Joyce, Mann, Kafka,
your mind darted sharply,
like a rainbow trout in stream,
seeking its nourishment
but at times impatient
as if hurry were thought.
Bright, engaging, you bestrode
college like a Colossus,
never quite separating performance from living.

II.

When I told my sons that
I taught Superman how to fly,
you still occupied a corner of my mindscape.
It piqued my vanity's palette
that you singled me out
during campus visit two years ago.
I took unreasonable pride
in your public adoration,
preened myself
that in some oblique way,
I had infinitesimal influence.

III.

Who would have thought that I,
a generation older,
would be running, swimming,
while you,
thrown from your horse,
would be saying:
"There is more to me than my body."

IV.

Vacationing far from my moorings,
walking among sea oats,
wandering on fishing dock,
exchanging stories with folks
with whom I have only in common
love of fishing,
forgetting momentarily
issues of mortality,
father's aging,
sons' efforts to find a way, a place,
I discover handsome smile, blue eyes
staring past Barbara Walters at me.
Between sentences you gasp, and
arm-like tubes embrace you
like mechanical octopus
enveloping elaborate chair
designed to support muscle atrophy.

Elegy for Elizabeth Rose Lane Galloway

May 7, 1997–May 9, 1997

We stood on gray
May day in cemetery,
each lost in past griefs,
trying to make sense of child's
life lasting two days.
A tiny, closed white casket,
standing in for her damaged body—
stopped breath, silent cry—
speaks to our inability to articulate grief
for a beginning that was an end.

Grief, too, has a lineage.
I hear her father's quivering whisper—
"We have had a tragedy"—
my mind's eye reverts to
weeping for friend's baby
who fatally fell from his crib
months after my infant son
had tumbled down
concrete stairs,
barely scathed.

I see my younger self, eulogizing Paul,
devoured by cancer,
giving way to grayer version
celebrating gentle George
killed three years ago
in conflagration of steel and bone.
Shivering in the graveyard,
I almost feel inevitable

ring in the night
tolling for one or other
of my frail parents.

Death's rites have their own geography,
staking a claim to place in our memory.
Obsequies become map
we use to explore our terrain.
For me, late spring has become death's season.
As shriveled daffodils give way to tulips,
geese and ducks return to pond,
kingfishers resume their predatory watch,
lone heron stands proudly
guarding rotting tree stump,
mortality's arrow quivers in my flesh.

Generations

January 1, 2000

We celebrated New Years Day with
generation older than ourselves.
Time, ghostly uninvited
guest, circulated like
stale medicated air in hospice room.
Conversational hum and buzz
touched by mortality
returned me to my past, even as
I saw my future self:
stooped bodies bent by time,
hearing aids, flaccid skin, canes,
wrinkled faces whose geographic
lines mapped worthy histories.

A warm touching occasion:
men and women I once
held in awe, who were my current age or
younger when I first arrived in Ithaca,
bursting with elegiac murmurs:
"She is in its worst stage, the time
when one knows one is caught
in its inexorable grip,"
grieved a luminary
of his still elegant wife now
ravaged by Alzheimer's.
A few guests huddled
in corner, sharing the pain
of adult children lost to heroin,
alcohol, and mental collapse.

Caught in warp of
another time, greeting me warmly
yet feigning full recognition,
others insinuated intimacy that never was,
as if I were bridge to
younger world they once knew.
Some never appeared, debilitated by illness,
loss of faculties, though present in
to and fro of regrets, memories, elegies.
Yet I imagined them as they were,
in full vigor, at similar parties years ago,
and realized I will be them,
my sons me, and the yet unborn
would watch my sons age.

Cancer: The Uninvited Guest

arrives unwelcome
lurking in dark corners
of our bodily rooms.
It puts life on fast forward,
has its own grim time:
Cancer Standard Time
in which each day
becomes precious gift,
yet space for helpless rage.
Gradually, cancer puts on its
masque, harlequin
from commedia dell'arte,
becomes flush spot, bald spot,
devours girth around waist.
It masquerades as dark spots on
X-rays, flush or pale spots on face,
hollow cavities, cough,
even as it assumes other roles:
disfiguring grimace,
gnarled bent posture,
amputation.

IX. Briefly: Haiku

Nature

Spring, 2005

Awestruck, I beheld
Goldfinches, dancing birches,
birthing catkins, leaves.

Daylight Savings Time

Suggests spring's bright blooms,
promises fecundity,
ripening berries.

Strawberries

Ripe fragility,
succulent juice on palate:
tinctures, stains, regrets.

After the 2/8/13 Snow

Snowshoeing: crisp, bright
morning air in unspoiled woods,
our steps the first tracks.

Spring's Promise: Walking in Woods

Tracking through damp brush,
stunned by bluebird's bright beauty,
buds ready to burst.

Questions of Travel

Homage to Elizabeth Bishop

Flying

Soft clouds pillow planes;
floating forward, passengers
seeking flight from self.

International Travel

Hermetically
sealed in our separateness,
jetting oceans, worlds.

Istanbul

Throngs hustle, bustle.
Abstract patterns decorate
carpets, bazaars, mosques.

Santorini (I)

Perched on Fira's cliffs
overlooking volcanic isles:
glorious sunsets.

Santorini (II)

Black volcanic rock
sets off flaming red sunset
perched above ocean.

Alaska

Stark, snow-capped mountains,
roaring of calving glaciers,
moose, grizzly sightings.

Mendenhall Glacier

Sublime Mendenhall:
stark immensity of ice,
blue tonality.

High Meadow, Keene Valley

Mountain spectacle:
High Peaks in Adirondacks,
Twilight, pied skyscape.

Keene Valley

Brooks, creeks, lakes: soaring
evergreens delight our eyes.
Mist masks higher peaks.

Perspectives

Achievements by Others

Recognition pricks
self-doubting humans, spreading
jealousy's green rash.

Pantomime

We best know ourselves
in silences, deft gestures—
and are known by them.

Folly

He once thought his life
could have the splendor of a
Raphael cartoon.

Fractured Expectations

Fabric: faded hopes,
once taut threads of woven plans
now unraveling.

X. The Mind's Garden: Imaginative Journeys

Travel

is for me hermetic,
an ordering: each trip
a life, with its own defined
beginning and ending,
an escape from
thick textures
of adult life: heavy weights
of work and relationships.
Travel is world
out of time:
anxieties controlled,
mortality put off,
attention distracted.
Travel is oasis,
abbreviated lifetime,
sealing world
from intrusion,
creating space
of two spare,
bare weeks.

Looking Backwards at Eighty-Two: Anecdotes of Light and Dark

These fragments I have shored against my ruins.
    —T.S. Eliot, *The Waste Land*

Winter's short sunless days
open trove of memories:
joys, sorrows.
We live in our minds' spaces
which expand to
comforting circles,
contract to painful points.

Marble-white Taj Mahal,
Mughal mausoleum.
First tourists at dawn:
looming majestic presence
shimmers in light, emerging
slowly from morning haze.

Arabian Sea, Goa:
swimming naked,
pure red sunrise
flaming/framing
my wife's back.
All I can say:
"Look behind you."

Cambodian Temples.
Scorching noon sun:
grandeur, harmony.

Seven-headed Naga causeway
leads to Angkor Wat's
bas-relief friezes,
Eastern gallery alive
with Hindu Creation myth:
churning sea of milk.

Victoria Lodge, Zimbabwe:
sun slowly setting
over Zambezi River:
herd of Cape Buffalo
crossing single file
approaching pond.
In ceremonious sync,
loudly trumpeting elephants
one by one arrive
perpendicular
to departing buffaloes.

If sublime belongs to
mind's circle, sorrows
belong to mind's point.

Moving out at night,
accompanied by
cherished books,
much-worn clothing,

after marriage capsized in
storms of self-interest,
winds of misunderstanding.

Watching mother
capitulate to mortality:
she lay diminished,
shrunken by illness
in dark hospital room,
I helpless to intervene.

Aging: malaise, anxiety
gnaws at mind's edges.
Yet memory summons
sustaining splendors.

Possessions

I sit among fragments
of different cultures,
maps of travels,
benediction of middle years,
culled from probing journeys:
elaborate woven patterns of Hereke carpet,
Torajan wall hanging,
cloisonné from China, Bohemian cut glass,
Inuit soapstone depicting a mythical
creature half human, half seal;
Mexican stone carving,
snake devouring its own tail;
carved female statue
from New Guinea's Sepik River,
weathered African masks.
These are shards, too,
of who I am.

Reading Dante's *The Divine Comedy*

*Midway in our life's journey, I went astray
from the straight road and woke to find myself
alone in a dark wood. How shall I say
what wood that was! I never saw so drear,
so rank, so arduous a wilderness!
Its very memory gives a shape to fear.*
—Dante Alighieri, *The Divine Comedy,* Canto 1
   John Ciardi's translation

Across seven centuries,
Dante's narrative speaks.
If I doubt a path to Heaven,
I have experienced life's journey.
If Hell is a state of mind—disappointments,
spats, haunting memories of
occasions when I could
have done better, anxiety, self-doubt,
terrifying fear of aging, trembling in face of
what awaits—have I not been there?
"Death could scarce be more bitter than that place!"

If Purgatory is a testing time when
one, alive to natural beauties,
lives in vestibule of uncertainly,
waits for recognition, learns humility,
sorts out values, comes to terms
with shortcomings, overcomes selfishness,
grapples with misunderstanding,
stews in regrets, accepts who we are—
—and who we are not—knows
that body is failing,
learns about generosity,
forgiveness, I have lived those
healing, restorative ways, days.

Paradise for me is not heavenly bliss.
Rather satisfying moments
between tick and tock,
what my body can still do
at eighty, small pleasures of each day,
finding sustenance, stability
in loving others, being loved,
memories of significant moments:
satisfying accomplishments,
special conversations, shared intimacy,
recollected moments of awe.
India: tigers, leopards.
Antarctica: snow, penguins, elephant seals.
Masai-Mara: wildebeest, zebra migration.
Completing our circle:
just as we learn from Virgil and Dante,
so we become teachers,
sharing magic gifts of
imagination: reading, writing.
A nuance of Paradise is joy in
having made students' lives
ever so slightly better,
watching them take their place
in the world, perhaps in my best days
demonstrating examples of empathy, decency.

Reading Joyce's *Ulysses*

*Force, hatred, history, all that. That's not life
for men and women, insult and hatred.*

*I belong to a race, too . . . that is hated
and persecuted. Also now. This very moment.
This very instant.*
                    —James Joyce, *Ulysses*

Bloom's Jewish heritage
pulsates through his veins;
he feels exile, diasporic pain.
Despite assimilation,
compromise, tolerance, he
speaks boldly to such
one-eyed monsters
as Citizen Cyclops.
St. Leopold of Perpetual Responsibility,
Lamed Vov (Just Man),
visiting Mrs. Purefoy in her labor,
caring for the widow Dignam,
loving Molly,
at once his Calypso and Penelope.
Living with hope of return,
willfully ignoring
the Blazing disruption
of Eccles Street home,
haunted by pentimento of
father's suicide, infant son's
death; guilt and loss are
etched into his flesh like a tattoo.
His scars are psychic scars,
like ones we all bear.
His Hades, like ours, is within:

fears, obsessions,
dimly acknowledged needs.
He, too, is teacher;
his subject is humanity.
He is Stephen's Nestor
but also his Virgil,
accompanying him and, yes, us,
through divinely human comedy.

About Suffering

a response to W.H. Auden's "Musée des Beaux Arts"

About suffering they could be wrong,
The Old Masters: when and if they ignored
effects of massacres,
cries of mothers who
have lost their kin and kind,
when and if they could not imagine
paranoid fantasies triggering
psychotic explosive acts:
fingers wedded to guns,
perambulatory mindbombs.
For every Guernica,
there has been sound of silence.
Take Picasso's Occupation days:
did he notice when
friend Max Jacobs disappeared?
Bosnia, Rwanda, Somalia, Israel, Gaza:
Massacre of Innocents
is everywhere, takes many forms.
While Icarus drops from sky,
others lose parents, children, hope.

Cézanne in Philadelphia

1996

Today I collected my inheritance
from Cézanne's estate.
I behold draughtsman's
hand mysteriously drawing with
fat luscious swathes of sensuous
shapes and colors, transforming
sketches into illuminations,
travelling into imaginative
space, insisting that we see.
I meet my guide in the first room:
skeptical imposing *Uncle
Dominic*—left eye raised—becomes
my Virgil, as he might have been Cézanne's.
Vernacular motif: raptly
intent card players, punctuated
regularly by deft psychological
probings of stolid, geometric Madame
Cézanne. Personality, even character,
disappears in search for perfect
arrangement of floating forms in *The Bathers:*
woman and trees become interchangeable
shapes with anonymous
roofs in small Provence village.
Sudden shift: red-brown earth color
intrudes, is taken up, played with,
reinscribed elsewhere; asparagus-shaped trees:
verticals reaching passionately skyward.
Millstone in the Park of the Chateau:
debris of an abandoned mill,
discarded building stone, loose rocks,

millstone. Cézanne's final
journey to abstraction: geometric
forms, blurred, contoured;
blotches, swabs, dabs of color, surprising
shadows, efficiency of line,
distortions ordering perceptions.
Yes, I beheld Cézanne for the first
time today. When I drove home, the
foggy evening drew shapes,
colors into new patterns,
and I saw afresh.

Picasso's Women

Marie Thérèse, earth mother:
passionate sensuous images
evoking children blowing bubbles,
romping on sand,
gently swaying to Antibes breezes—
blissful memories set to gentle music.
Take *Girl before a Mirror:*
fantastic double image,
insistent wedding of opposites,
her head a marvel of compression,
half hidden frontal view becomes
a cosmetic mask of sexual allure,
evocation of astronomical rhythms.

But it is otherwise with Dora Maar:
grimacing, swollen face,
convulsive postures,
weeping woman, cadaver,
disfigured, monstrous;
the macabre 1940 *Head of a Woman;*
a skull grits its teeth in rage.

Seated Woman: Françoise's inquiring visage,
fecund body, staring eyes, forcefully seated.
Woman-Flower: blossoming form
sheds its mass; her slim, oval
body like the stalk and bloom of a sunflower.
Her blue tonality injects a lunar coolness,
counterpointing the woman as flower,
reminding us of Picasso's conversation—and ours—
with visible and invisible worlds.

On (Re)Reading Tolstoy's *War and Peace*

Living with Rostovs and Boronskys
for several weeks as I again
wend my way through
early nineteenth century Tsarist Russia;
over twelve hundred pages
open door to genius:
loves, disappointments,
losses, grievings.
History as serendipity:
compilation of grammar of
motives, physical gestures,
coalescing retrospectively
into perceived patterns.

Obese, cuckolded, bumbling,
gauche, puzzled, questing
Pierre overcomes his faults,
winning our sympathy
with his simplicity,
decency, lack of guile,
heartfully loving Natasha.

Rereading Conrad's *Heart of Darkness*

"Mistah Kurtz—he dead."
—Joseph Conrad, *Heart of Darkness*

We prefer games with rules,
red and black pieces, even
mazes, conundrums,
rather than uncontrollable, unseen
darkness lurking within.
When we had hoped
to find mere banality,
discovery of inexplicable
terrifying evil and mindless
violence frightens;
we don't want to deal
with severed heads
or the stench of
buried hippo,
real or metaphoric.

An idealist armed
with values of his culture,
Kurtz reverts to racism, savagery.
Indifferent to elephants, humans,
his one-minded quest for ivory
is cursed with ferocious
accumulating impulse.
Is "The horror! The horror!"
his moment of self-recognition,
or cry of a dying
megalomaniac whose hopes
are checkmated?

Fascinated, hypnotized
by Kurtz as an alternative
to imperialistic pawns,
does not Marlow go
ashore for "a howl and a dance?"
When Kurtz escapes, Marlow stalks
him in the jungle as if he were his prey
before confronting the danger in himself,
rediscovering moral track he almost lost.
Like Gulliver, he returns
shadowed, checked,
yet enlightened by experience.
We readers, too.

XI. Conclusion

Fragrant Portals

Words of the fragrant portals, dimly starred,
And of ourselves and of our origins,
In ghostlier demarcations, keener sounds.
   —Wallace Stevens, "The Idea of Order at Key West"

I live in words,
savoring their
sensuality, tactility,
tastes, smells, sounds.
Given verbal shape,
memories become reality.
Walking alone in woods,
words jump into head,
responding to
inchoate experience
with sentences I can see
before I write them,
evoking places, people,
emotions, hopes, dreams.

About the Author

Daniel R. Schwarz (1941–) is Frederic J. Whiton Professor of English Literature and Stephen H. Weiss Presidential Fellow at Cornell University, where he has taught since 1968. He is a renowned teacher, scholar, and public intellectual. In 1998, he received Cornell's College of Arts and Sciences Russell award for distinguished teaching. In 1999 he received the Weiss title, which is Cornell's most esteemed teaching honor.

Since 2009, Schwarz has been Faculty President of the Cornell chapter of Phi Beta Kappa. He has been the longtime Faculty Advisor to the Literary Society and House Fellow at Rose House, one of Cornell's five residential colleges. Schwarz's fifty years at Cornell were celebrated with a two-day conference entitled "Celebrating Dan Schwarz: Fifty Years of Transformative Teaching," attended by several hundred of his former students.

Schwarz has directed nine NEH seminars and lectured widely in the United States and abroad, including a number of lecture tours under the auspices of the academic programs of the USIS and State Department. He has held three endowed visiting professorships and been a Guest Fellow for short periods at Oxford and Cambridge.

He is author of the well-received *Endtimes? Crises and Turmoil at the New York Times, 1999–2009* (Excelsior Edition of SUNY Press, 2012; paperback edition with a new preface, 2014). He has written on the media and higher education for *The Huffington Post*. His book on undergraduate education, *How to Succeed in College and Beyond: The Art of Learning* (2017–18), has had a wide circulation and been translated into Mandarin for an edition published in China.

Schwarz is a leading authority on James Joyce, Joseph Conrad, twentieth-century Modernism, and theory of the novel as well as on humanistic and pluralistic approaches to literature. Also an authority on the Holocaust, he has recently published *The Story in Fiction and Film of French Collaboration in the Occupation and Complicity in the Holocaust (1940–1944)*.

His more recent scholarly books are *Reading the European Novel to 1900* (2014) and *Reading the Modern European Novel since 1900* (2018–2019). His books include *In Defense of Reading: Teaching Literature in the Twenty-First Century* (2008) in the prestigious Blackwell Manifesto series; *Broadway Boogie Woogie: Damon Runyon and the Making of New York City Culture* (2003); and *Imagining the Holocaust* (1999).

He has edited Joyce's *The Dead* (1994) and Conrad's *The Secret Sharer* (1997) in the Bedford Case Studies in Contemporary Criticism Series. He served as Consulting Editor of the six-volume edition of *The Early Novels of Benjamin Disraeli* (2004), for which he wrote the General Introduction. He is General Editor of the multi-volume critical series *Reading the Novel,* for which he wrote *Reading the Modern British and Irish Novel, 1890–1930* (2004) and a two-volume study of the European Novel.

His interests include travel, art museums, theatre, ballet, music, tennis, fishing, long walks, and swimming. He has published over a hundred poems as well as numerous articles on current events, higher education, and travel.

View his work at:
courses.cit.cornell.edu/drs6/

www.ingramcontent.com/pod-product-compliance
Lightning Source LLC
Chambersburg PA
CBHW022142160426
43197CB00009B/1399